I used to play football.

...I would teach my younger self about how to manage money.

Because when I was young, I used to spend...

... and spend and SPEND my money...all the time!

I would buy all the food I wanted.

"What's a budget?" my younger self would ask.

"A budget is a plan for saving and spending your money." I would answer. "You shouldn't spend all of your money at once, even though you want to."

"Every time you get some money, you should make a plan to divide it into each of these buckets. Save some money, spend some money, and give some money away. This is a good plan to follow."

"Or you can use your SAVE money to go to school."

"Then, you can put some money in your SPEND jar. This is money that you can spend on whatever you want!"

"But, you have to decide what is a NEED and what is a WANT. A NEED is something that you need to survive, like food and water. If you have shoes with big holes, a need would be new shoes..."

"You have to decide which one is more important, and then spend your money on that thing. Maybe you choose to SAVE for the other things later!"

"The last jar is a GIVE jar. This jar is for you to put aside money so that you can help others or give to a church or community organization."

"The GIVE jar reminds you that everyone needs help sometimes, and that you can make a big difference in somebody's life with the money in your GIVE jar."

"That's all cool, but how do I earn money?"
"That's a good question, Little Ken!"

"You can work and earn money by doing things like mowing lawns, babysitting, and walking dogs. You can also get a job after you graduate from school. There are a lot of ways to make money!"

"So, does this make sense, little Ken?"
"Yes it does! Thanks for teaching me about budgeting!"

"Great! Now I will go check on the older you to see if you got it!"

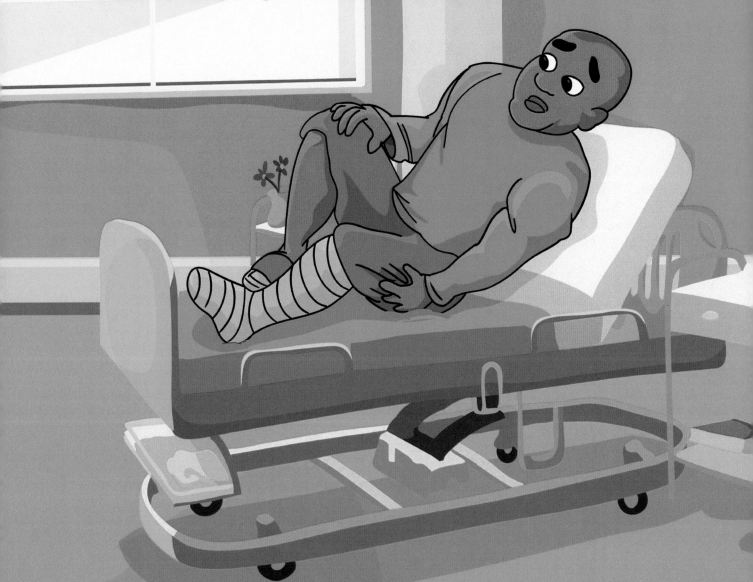

"Are you sure, Football Player Ken? What if you get hurt? What if you hadn't made it to the pros? Then what? Saving money is important so that it's there for you JUST IN CASE."

The End

My name is

_____

(write your name here)

and I promise to become the Me that Needs to Be!

SAVE/SPEND/GIVE

This book is dedicated to the parents of all young children.
Plant the seeds of knowledge and teach them well.

-Ken Harvey

Owl Publishing

717-925-7511

www.owlpublishinghouse.com

Copyright text © 2020 Ken Harvey

ISBN-13: 978-1-949929-58-4

Library of Congress Control Number- In production

Made in the USA
Middletown, DE
17 December 2020